# We Are The Champions

*Jokes by six of the best young jokesters*

compiled and edited by
Jan Needle

illustrated by Graham Humphreys

**A Piccolo Original**
Piccolo Books

What's classy, plays the
banjo, and gets run
down by trucks?

My friend
Carole Docherty
to whom this masterpiece
is dedicated

First published 1984 by Pan Books Ltd,
Cavaye Place, London SW10 9PG
9 8 7 6 5 4 3 2
This collection © Jan Needle 1984
Illustrations © Graham Humphreys 1984
ISBN 0 330 28143 7
Phototypeset by Input Typesetting Ltd, London
Printed and bound in Great Britain by
Hunt Barnard Printing, Aylesbury, Bucks

# We Are The Champions

# CHALLENGE

Well, do you think you can beat the champions? If you do, why not send your best jokes to Jan Needle at the address below?

It's not easy, though. You'll have to send AT LEAST FIFTY, and they'll have to be good, different, and not just taken from various books (especially not this one!).

Think you have a chance? Get inventing, adapting, collecting. You too might one day be a
CHAMPION

Send your Jokes to:
Jan Needle
c/o Piccolo Books
Pan Books Ltd
Cavaye Place, London SW10 9PG

# New readers begin here . . .

When I was a boy – and I was once, despite my name – I had a friend called Hairpin who was a walking comedy show. If we saw a bike leaning against a wall he'd reveal that it couldn't stand up because it was two-tyred. If we saw a plane in the sky he'd say: 'Why is flying like a deadly poison? Because one drop kills you!' And it was he who told me that stealing a pair of gloves was known to the police as 'committen a crime . . . '.

'Jokes are funny things,' he used to say (and it's not the sort of remark I could ever think of an answer to), 'because everyone knows them, but nobody knows where they come from.'

In my case he was half right and half wrong. He was wrong because although I loved jokes I never knew any. Or at least, I did, but I always messed them up in the telling. I was the sort of twit who said things like: 'Why couldn't the church steeple keep a secret – because the bell always rang' (it should have been 'tolled'!). And he was right because I didn't have the foggiest idea where they came from. Except from him.

Before I got smart enough to think of asking Hairpin where jokes *did* come from, and if he made all his up, his family emigrated to Australia. There was a rumour for a while that they were going to leave him behind, because they couldn't stand his jokes, or even that the Australian Government wouldn't let him in for the same reason. ('How do witches travel in the Outback?' he asked me. 'By broomerang!') But sadly, it was not true. He did send me a card once, with a picture of a rabbit on it (it came by hare-mail, of course). But I never saw him again.

Ever since those far-off days, I've been an avid collector of jokes; and some time ago, by one of those strokes of luck that even men with women's names have from time to time, I was asked to be the children's editor of a national newspaper. This was probably because I write children's books, some of which – like *The Size Spies, Another Fine Mess, Losers Weepers* and *Rottenteeth* – are comedies which lots of people (not just me for once!) reckon to be a laugh. The nicest thing about the job was that children from all over Britain – for a small financial consideration, naturally – kept sending me jokes. Which strangely enough, brings me back to Hairpin.

The thing was, it quickly became clear that, although thousands of people knew *some* jokes, all the best ones seemed to come from the same small group of children – over and over again. Like my old mate, they were the champions. And the six who appear in this book – Adrian Bealing, Nichola Lynch, Julie Filer, Darren Giles, Julie Stopford, and Melanie Giles – were among the very best of the very best. What's more, I discovered when I got in touch with them, that at least some of them *did* make jokes up themselves. Another part of the mystery was solved! This book is a collection of some of their favourites, followed by some of mine. If you think you could do better when you've read it – there's a challenge on Page 1.

PS. I'm very fond of silly facts, as well. Did you know, for instance, that during the First World War Americans used to kick dachshunds on sight because of anti-German feeling? Or that Florence Nightingale always carried a pet owl in her pocket, even during the Crimean War? Or that ants have five noses? (Except eleph-ants of course, which have only one – but very long! Groogh!) Or that Nelson was seasick *every time* he went to sea? Or that Ancient Romans used to like a snack of dormice from time to time?

I bet you didn't – so I've put in a few to break up the jokes. But I warn you, they're not the sort of facts your teacher will give you marks for knowing!

Have fun.

JAN NEEDLE

Second PS. Thanks also to Angus McEwan, of Glasgow, and Steven Prytherch – last heard of somewhere near Wigan. They helped too.

# Adrian Bealing's Jokes

Adrian Bealing is fourteen, lives in Southend, Essex, and goes to Thorpe Bay High School. He has been collecting jokes 'for ages', and reckons to get five or six good ones in a week 'if I'm lucky'.

Even when he's not lucky, though, Adrian makes up and adapts jokes all the time. He has worked it out that about half the jokes he tells come mainly from his own head. He tests them out on his Dad, who's called Rod – and 'if he laughs, I know they're all right'. He also tries out jokes at school, and improves the ones that don't work so well. He has done a 'turn' with some friends at the school concert – and 'to our great surprise the audience laughed'.

Adrian's hobbies are judo, cricket, entering competitions (a couple of wins so far – all the family share the prizes) and jokes. When he's older he 'wouldn't mind having a bash at being a comic – but I'll certainly try gag-writing for other comedians'.

His sister Sharron, who also goes to Thorpe Bay, collects jokes as well. Sample: What's green and careers round lamp-posts? A mad cabbage! She finds that people don't laugh at the jokes she thinks are the funniest!

I know the feeling . . .

●

What lies in a pram and wobbles?

A jelly baby.

●

What kind of sandals do frogs wear?

Open-toad.

What do you get if you cross a racehorse with a giraffe?

> An animal that's very hard to ride, but great in a photo-finish.

•

How do you know when you're eating rabbit stew?

> It's got hares in it.

•

Why is being in hospital a good laugh?

> Because the surgeons have you in stitches.

Why don't pigs telephone each other?

  There's too much crackling on the line.

•

What do you call the fleas on a parrot?

  Politics.

•

What's white and fluffy, has whiskers, and floats?

  A catameringue.

•

Why does Superman wear gumboots?

  Because his Dad flew in Wellingtons during the war.

•

What are a dentist's four favourite letters of the alphabet?

  I.C.D.K.

•

Where do pigs go for their holidays?

Nowhere, they sty at home.

●

How does an Eskimo make his house stand up?

Igloos it together.

●

What's grey and comes at you from all sides?

Stereophonic porridge.

●

What do you get if you cross a citrus fruit with a bell?

An orange that can peal itself.

●

If you find gold in goldmines, where do you find Silver?

Under the Lone Ranger.

●

Why are bananas never lonely?

Because they hang around in bunches.

●

Why is Dracula poor?

Because he's always in the red.

●

'Doctor doctor, I keep thinking I'm an elastic band.'
'Just take your clothes off and stretch out on that couch.'

●

How does Jack Frost go to work?

By-icicle.

●

What car is popular in China?

A Rolls Rice.

●

Who invented gunpowder?

A lady who wanted guns to look pretty.

●

'Doctor doctor, I keep thinking I'm a pound note.'
'Go out shopping, the change will do you good.'

●

What would you call Dracula's boat?

A blood vessel.

●

Why did the farmer fail his driving test?

He couldn't make a ewe turn.

●

What do you call a mad spaceman?

An astronut.

●

What does a nuclear scientist have for lunch?

Fission chips.

•

Who lives in the desert and invented
flavoured crisps?

Sultan Vinegar.

•

'How long have you been bald, Dad?'
'Since the war, son. I lost it in a hair raid.'

•

What do you call a man who steals cattle?

A beefburglar.

●

What do you call a man whose life is in ruins?

An archaeologist.

●

Why do nuns wear black?

It's a habit they get into.

●

Did you hear about the clergyman who turned up at the wrong funeral?

He made a grave mistake.

●

What is a meatball?

A dance in a butcher's shop.

●

What did the cannibal say to the famous missionary?

Doctor Livingstone, I consume.

What did Mozart do when he was buried?

Decomposed.

What go squeak-squeak when you pour milk over them?

Mice crispies.

What can speak in any language?

An echo.

What do you get if you cross a Jeep and a dog?

A Land Rover.

Why is a pork pie hat uncomfortable to wear?

Because the gravy runs down your neck.

What do you get if you cross a bee with a giant ape?

Sting Kong.

What did the flour say when it fell off the table?

> Don't pick me up, I'm self-raising.

•

Why is Sunday the strongest day?

> Because the others are weak days.

•

What do you call a judge with no fingers?

> Justice Thumbs.

•

Why shouldn't you phone people before they get married?

> They'll probably be engaged.

•

What are pig skins used for?

> Holding pigs together.

•

Why do people cry at weddings?

> Well, the cake's always in tiers!

What do you call the toilet at a zoo?

    A zulu.

•

Why was Beethoven always laughing?

    Because everything symphony to him.

•

Why didn't Beethoven trust anybody?

    Because they all symphony to him.

•

(These two jokes are Adrian Bealing specials.
Terrible!)

•

How do you stop meatballs from drowning?

    Put them in gravy boats.

•

If moonbeams hold up the moon and
sunbeams hold up the sun, what holds up
Mars?

    Mars bars!

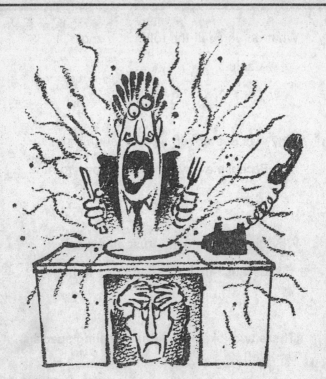

Where would you find exploding spaghetti?

At the Minestrone of Defence.

•

Why does everything go wrong in Moscow?

Because the Gremlin's there!

•

What do you feed a starving parrot?

Polyfilla.

In the 1660s, every child in hospital in Norwich was allowed two gallons of beer a week.

It is still an offence to use a Royal Coat of Arms without permission. The maximum penalty is death – by beheading!

# Nichola Lynch's Jokes

Nichola Lynch is ten, lives in Wrexham, North Wales, and goes to Rhosddu Junior School. She makes up a lot of her own jokes as well as adapting the ones she hears and reads. She tries them out on Mum and Dad (Marge and Ron). Marge says she has been making people laugh ever since she could string a sentence together.

Nichola also does impersonations, party pieces, and funny 'turns' for the relations. She thinks it helps having an Irish Dad! She sends her jokes all over the place, and any money she wins goes to her 'dream fund' – she wants to visit Disney World in Florida.

Her hobbies are dancing (ballet and tap),

gymnastics, the Brownies, roller skating, swimming, playing the organ and the recorder, and reading.

When she grows up she would like to be a ballet dancer or, failing that, a journalist. She also writes short stories and would like to write gags for comedians. She has a six-year-old sister called Sharleen.

●

What is the best Christmas present you can give?

A drum takes a lot of beating.

●

How do you confuse an Eskimo boy who has been naughty?

Tell him to stand in the corner of his igloo.

●

Who is the biggest lady in America?

Mrs Sippy.

●

Why is it hard to fool a snake?

Because he has no leg to pull.

●

What game do horses play?

Stable tennis.

●

What is white and fluffy and flies through the air?

A meringue-outang.

●

Why does a dog wag its tail?

Because no one else will wag it for him.

●

What bus crossed the Atlantic Ocean?

Columbus.

●

What is the best way to catch a squirrel?

Climb up a tree and act like a nut.

What is the definition of a skeleton?

Bones with the people scraped off.

●

What is another name for beans on toast?

Skinheads on a raft.

●

Why is a black chicken smarter than a white chicken?

Because a black chicken can lay a white egg but a white chicken can't lay a black one.

●

What happened to the man who said he was listening to the match?

He burnt his ear.

●

What is red, black and white and driven by policemen?

A sunburnt panda.

●

What do you get if you cross an elephant with a mouse?

>Extra large holes in the skirting board and a trunkful of cheese.

Why does a stork stand on one leg?

>Because if he didn't he'd fall over.

Why did the boy take a pencil to bed?

>To draw the curtains.

'Doctor doctor, I keep seeing striped camels!'
'Have you ever seen a psychiatrist?'
'No, only striped camels.'

●

'Doctor doctor, I keep thinking I'm a dustbin!'
'Don't talk rubbish.'

●

Tom: 'Do you believe in free speech?'
Dick: 'I certainly do.'
Tom: 'Good, can I use your telephone?'

●

Dentist: 'What kind of filling do you want in your teeth?'
Johnny: 'How about chocolate or marshmallow!'

●

How did the blind carpenter regain his sight?

He picked up his hammer and saw.

●

What do astronauts like in their sandwiches?

Launcheon meat.

•

What do you call a baby whale that's crying?

A little blubber.

•

A postman walked into a hospital and said a dog had just bitten his leg.
'Did you put anything on it?' asked the nurse.
'No,' he replied. 'He liked it just as it was!'

•

Auntie: 'Dick, why are you scratching yourself?'
Dick: 'No one else knows where I itch!'

•

Man: 'Ouch! A crab just bit my toe!'
Friend: 'Which one?'
Man: 'I don't really know – all crabs look alike to me.'

•

Why did the egg go into the jungle?

Because it wanted to be a famous eggsplorer.

Doctor: 'Put your tongue out at that window.'
Patient: 'Will that help me?'
Doctor: 'Not at all – but I hate the man who lives opposite!'

'Teacher, teacher, Tommy has swallowed 50p!'
Teacher: 'Oh, that's all right. It was his dinner money.'

●

What do you call a Christmas play about ghosts?

A phanto.

●

What do hedgehogs eat with bread and cheese?

Prickled onions.

●

Patient: 'If this swelling on my leg gets any bigger, I won't be able to get my trousers on.'
Doctor: 'That's all right. Here's a prescription for a kilt.'

●

Why do wizards drink tea?

Because sorcerers need cuppas.

What football team have never met before
the game?

Queen's Park Strangers.

•

What do you call a flea on the moon?

A lunartick.

•

What do Italian ghosts have for dinner?

Spooketti.

•

'Doctor, doctor, I keep thinking I'm a parrot.'
'Just perch yourself there – I'll tweet you in
a minute!'

•

'Doctor, doctor, I've just swallowed my
camera!'
'Oh dear – let's hope nothing serious
develops.'

•

Why are big people lazier than small people?

They lie longest in bed.

•

How do you start a pudding race?

Sago!

•

Doctor: 'I'm afraid you've only got three
minutes left to live.'
Man: 'Is there nothing you can do for me?'
Doctor: 'I could boil you an egg.'

•

Where do wasps come from?

Stingapore.

•

What haunts a seaside cafe?

A sandwitch!

•

What do you get if you cross Larry Grayson,
a Red Indian, and Tommy Cooper?

Shut that door! How? Just like that!

•

What do you call an Irish spider?

Paddy Longlegs.

•

How does a robot sit?

Bolt upright.

•

What fish performs serious operations?

A sturgeon!

•

'Waiter, waiter, how long will my spaghetti
be?'
'No idea sir – we never measure it.'

•

What are Scandinavian lovers called?

Swedehearts!

•

Where do you find an elastic band?

Playing at a rubber ball.

What do you call a highwayman with flu?

Sick Turpin.

Witch: 'I'm feeling much better today, doctor.'
Doctor: 'Good, you can get up for a spell this afternoon.'

•

How do you send a fisherman a letter?

Drop him a line.

•

Doctor: 'Why are you standing in that bowl?'
Patient: 'You told me to take these pills in water.'

•

Why did the woman get a shock when she picked up a bun?

The currant ran up her arm.

•

'Doctor, doctor, everything I swallow comes up!'
'Quick – swallow my football coupon!'

What do you get if you cross a kangaroo and a mink?

A fur coat with one big pocket

In 1725 a highwayman called Everet sued his partner in crime for not sharing the loot out fairly. But the judge just fined his solicitor – for impertinence in bringing the case!

Desert snails sometimes sleep for four years at a time!

# Julie Filer's Jokes

Julie Filer is fourteen, lives in Smethwick in the West Midlands and goes to Smethwick All Girls High School. She tries to make up her own jokes, 'but I've never made up a really good one'. Mostly she changes jokes to make them better. She gets them from other people, magazines, comics, and books.

'I try them out on my Mum, and I tell them to my friends,' said Julie. 'We're not really allowed to talk in class but I keep acting stupid and telling jokes.'

Her mother, Christine, pays for the postage for the competitions she enters.

'I've won quite a few prizes from local and national newspapers, including a Toyah double album. It's good,' she said.

Julie's hobbies are stamp-collecting, swimming and reading, and she loves animals. She has no brothers and sisters, but she's got a gerbil called Tiddleywink, which 'I talk to and so on'. Her ambition is to work with animals.

Favourite groups are Abba and Bucks Fizz. Favourite comedians: Cannon and Ball, Little and Large.

●

First tonsil: 'What are you getting all dressed up for?'
Second tonsil: 'Oh, the doctor's taking me out tonight!'

●

What is the quickest way to catch a fish?

Get someone to throw one at you.

●

What's grey and lumpy and weighs two tons?

A hippo with mumps.

●

What did the spider say to the fly?

> I'm getting married and you're invited to my webbing.

●

What do you call someone who's crazy about hot chocolate?

> A cocoanut!

●

What do you get when you cross a lunatic with a watch?

> A cuckoo clock.

●

What do you call a coat with no buttons or pockets?

> Paint.

●

How does a chick fit into an egg?

> Eggsactly.

●

Why can't you hold a conversation when there are goats around?

They always butt in.

•

Why are snakes careless?

They keep losing their skin.

•

What tree do you like best when you're hungry?

A pantry.

•

What happens when a shark swallows a bunch of keys?

He gets lockjaw.

•

What lives at the bottom of the sea and runs the Mafia?

The Codfather.

•

First kipper: 'Smoking is bad for you.'
Second kipper: 'It's all right, I've been cured.'

•

A man fell from the top of a twenty-storey building into a tank of lemonade – and wasn't hurt. Why?

It's a soft drink.

What's pink and dangerous and lives at the bottom of the sea?

Al Caprawn.

●

What ring is always square?

A boxing ring.

●

Why do people laugh up their sleeves?

Because that's where their funnybones are.

●

What does an elephant play in the back of a mini?

Squash.

●

What has three feet but cannot walk?

A yard.

●

What has more than three feet and sits under the stairs?

A meter!

●

What is Dracula?

He can be a pain in the neck.

●

Why can't farmers keep secrets?

> Because potatoes have eyes and corn has ears.

•

How do detectives hang up their washing?

> With clues pegs.

•

What do you call a knife that cuts four loaves at once?

> A four-loaf cleaver.

•

What do you call a stupid ape?

> A chumpanzee.

•

What dance do ducks like best?

> The quackstep.

•

How does one angel greet another?

> 'Halo there!'

What is black and white, black and white, black and white?

A penguin falling downstairs.

•

When is a telephone cold?

When it goes brrr-brrr.

•

Why did the cat eat cheese?

So that he could blow down the mousehole with baited breath.

•

If a man smashes a clock, can he be accused of killing time?

Not if the clock struck first!

•

When is the best time to pick apples?

When the farmer's not around.

•

A woman went to pay her rent with a £1 note in her left ear and a £5 note in her right ear. What state was she in?

Six pounds in arrears!

•

What do you call a fight between an Englishman and a Japanese man?

Punch and Judo!

•

Why is a banana like a dressing gown?

It's easy to slip on.

•

Shall I tell you the joke about the high wall?

I'd better not, you'll never get over it.

•

Why did the apple turnover?

Because it saw the Swiss roll.

•

What was Sir Galahad's favourite game?

Knights and crosses.

Why did the turkey cross the road?

Why did the turkey cross the road?

To prove he wasn't chicken.

•

What do you call a mad blackbird?

A raven lunatic.

•

What do polite lambs say to their mothers?

Thank ewe.

Where do you find giant snails?

> On giants' fingers.

●

What do you call a man wearing ear muffs?

> Anything you like – he can't hear you!

●

What is the most untidy part of a ship?

> The officers' mess.

●

Have you always been a dentist?

> No – I started as a chiropodist and
> worked my way up.

●

Why did the little brick cry?

> Because his mother was up the wall and
> his father was round the bend.

●

Why was the banker bored?

He'd lost interest.

•

How did the chimpanzee escape from his cage?

He used a monkey wrench.

•

What did the stove say to the pot?

I can make things hot for you.

•

What do the Australians call a very tough Englishman?

A pomegranite.

•

Where does a pig save his money?

In a piggy bank.

•

Why is an old car like a sausage?

Because it's a banger.

What happened to the cat that swallowed a ball of wool?

    She had mittens.

What did the whisky say when water was poured into the glass?

    I'm diluted to meet you.

Why is the person in charge of an orchestra like a piece of copper?

They are both good conductors.

•

What did the butcher say on the twelfth of December?

There aren't many chopping days left till Christmas.

•

What book has the most stirring chapters?

A cookery book.

•

What do you get if you cross a bald detective with a camera?

A Kojak instamatic.

•

Where do unlucky fiddlers spend the night?

In a vile inn.

•

When is cricket a crime?

When the players hit and run.

●

Why is the letter E lazy?

Because it can always be found in bed.

●

What goes all around a field but never moves?

A fence.

●

What do football fans sing at Christmas?

Yule never walk alone.

●

What bird helps you get to sleep?

A robin bed-rest.

●

How do you cut out the material for a Roman toga?

With a pair of caesars.

Where do spiders play football?

Webley Stadium.

●

What does a vicar do for exercise?

Hymnastics.

●

Which lady shouldn't you pick a fight with?

Madame Two Swords.

●

What is a ghost's favourite dessert?

Ice scream.

●

If a buttercup is yellow, what colour is a hiccup?

Burple.

●

Which Italian tourist attraction is famous for its taste?

The Leaning Tower of Pizza.

What kind of car would a greengrocer drive?

A peach buggy.

●

Why did the miser buy a black and white dog?

He thought the licence would be cheaper.

●

What goes quack quack and travels through time?

Ducktor Who.

●

What did the sign on the astronaut's door say?

Gone to launch.

●

What do you call a spaceman's watch?

A lunaticktock.

●

What's the nicest thing about being a fairy queen?

> You can have anything you wand.

●

What creature performs underwater operations?

> A doctopus.

●

What did Cinderella say when her photos were delayed at the chemist's?

> Some day my prints will come.

●

How does a bird land in an emergency?

> By sparrowchute.

●

What is a carpenter's favourite TV show?

> Plankety-plank.

●

How do you say sorry to an American
spaceman?

Apollo-gise.

•

What do you get if you cross Noel Edmonds
with a shirt factory?

The Multi-Collared Swap Shop.

*An Austrian who lived in the last century
designed a musical 'machine' that could be
played by one person, but reproduced the
sounds of 378 instruments. It did not catch
on.*

*The poet Virgil spent the equivalent of a
quarter of a million pounds burying a 'pet'
fly in his home. It was done to beat the
Roman tax law.*

# Darren Giles's Jokes

Darren Giles is fourteen, lives in Ampthill, Bedfordshire, and goes to Redborne Upper School. He collects about twenty-five good jokes a month, and tries them out on his Mum, Valerie – 'a good judge'. He reads a lot of joke books, and likes the *Dandy* and the *Beano*. Although he does not make up jokes himself, he changes them, 'I hope for the better'. He also has an uncle called Roger who gives him lots of good ones.

Darren's hobbies are snooker – he has a quarter-size table – and speedway. Weymouth are his favourite team, and he'd like to go and live there so that he could see them more often. He also likes fishing, football, rugby, and colouring. He has won quite a few competitions.

Why do they build ships on the River Clyde?

> Because if they built cars they would sink.

•

What do Scottish children have for pudding?

> Tartan custard.

•

Why don't bananas snore?

> They don't want to wake the rest of the bunch.

•

How do you make gold soup?

> Put in fourteen carrots.

•

What do you get if you cross a tape measure with a steamroller?

> Flat feet.

•

Why was the pixie told off by his mother?

> He was goblin his food.

How do you use an Egyptian doorbell?

Toot and come in.

•

What's the commonest illness in China?

Kung flu.

•

What kind of boat grants wishes?

A ferry godmother.

•

What is sharp and makes people sit up and take notice?

Income tacks.

•

What flies out of a wardrobe at 100 mph?

Stirling Moth.

•

What does a cat rest its head on?

A caterpillow.

What do you give an injured lemon?

Lemonaid.

•

Why is tennis a noisy game?

Because both players raise a racket.

•

Who was the youngest TV newsreader?

The one who read News at Ten.

•

What goes 'croak croak' in the mist?

A froghorn.

•

What do you get if you cross glass with a headache?

A window pane.

•

Who should be king of a small country?

A six-inch ruler.

What looks after a haunted stretch of beach?

The Ghost Guard.

•

What does a short-sighted ghost need?

Spooktacles.

What has twelve legs, three tails and cannot see?

> Three blind mice.

●

What is the weakest plant found in water?

> Seaweed.

●

What ate its victims two by two?

> Noah's shark.

●

What do you get if you cross a shellfish with a rocket warhead?

> A guided mussel.

●

What comes out of the sea at 1,000 mph?

> Another guided mussel!

●

Who invented King Arthur's table?

> Sir Cumference.

What is green and holds up stagecoaches?

Dick Gherkin.

•

What vegetable holds up stagecoaches and once rode to York on a horse called Black Bess?

Dick Turnip.

•

Who holds up stagecoaches, once rode to York on a horse called Black Bess, is not green, is not a vegetable, but is very good at removing paintstains?

Dick Turpentine.

•

Who was the Black Prince?

Old King Cole's son.

•

Where was King Solomon's temple?

On King Solomon's head.

•

Which fish is very musical?

A piano tuna.

How do kangaroos cross the Channel?

By hopper-craft.

What's big and bright but stupid as well?

A fool moon.

●

When can't astronauts land on the moon?

When it's full.

●

When is longhand quicker than shorthand?

On a clock.

●

Why is a boxer like a candle?

Because one good blow will put him out.

●

Who is as hard as nails and is always demanding money?

The tacks-man.

●

What happened to the cowboy who wore
paper trousers?

He was arrested for rustling.

•

How do you get the powers of a hypnotist?

Have a trance-plant.

•

What do you call a skeleton in a kilt?

Boney Prince Charlie.

•

Why did Dracula take medicine?

To cure his coffin.

•

Where do hedgehogs meet in London?

Prickadilly Circus.

•

Why is your nose in the middle of your face?

Because it is the scenter.

What do you call a dead man's nose?

The dead scenter!

•

What is the hottest letter of the alphabet?

B – it makes oil boil.

•

What athlete is warmest in winter?

A long jumper.

•

Why did the biscuit cry?

Because its mother was a wafer so long.

•

What would you get if you crossed a
snowball with a shark?

Frostbite.

•

How can a ghost go through a locked door?

By using a skeleton key.

What has four legs and flies?

Two pairs of trousers.

●

What do you call an underground train full
of university students?

A tube of smarties!

●

How can you recognise an undertaker?

By his grave manner.

●

What do they call a sky-diver from Helsinki?

A parafinn.

●

Who can shave three times a day and still
have a beard?

A barber.

●

What sort of song does a ghost like?

A haunting melody.

What do you call a baby whale?

A little squirt.

What is warm and tasty and found in the jungle?

Snake and pygmy pie.

What goes Da-dit-dit-croak, da-dit-da-croak?

Morse toad.

How can you tell which end of a worm is the head?

> Tickle the middle and see which end smiles.

●

How many feet in a yard?

> It depends on how many people are standing in it!

●

Where does Dracula keep his money?

> In a blood bank.

●

What grows shorter the older it gets?

> A lighted candle.

●

What is not much use until it's broken?

> An egg.

●

What belongs to you but is used more often by your friends?

Your name.

---

*Andrew Carnegie, one of the richest men ever, was once thrown off a London tram because he didn't have the fare!*

*The Queen's coronation date – 2 June 1953 – was specially chosen by weather experts. It rained.*

# Julie Stopford's Jokes

Julie Stopford is fourteen, lives in Blackpool, and goes to Highfield High School. She collects jokes from friends, magazines and comics, and adapts them if she can. She tries them out on her parents (Margaret and Alan) and on her friends. If everyone laughs she writes them down in a special book. If no one laughs, she throws them out! She has entered a few competitions, 'but I haven't won many yet'.

Her hobbies are swimming, reading, and collecting Bucks Fizz posters. Her favourite singers are Bucks Fizz and Shakin' Stevens. Favourite comics: Cannon and Ball and Little and Large.

Julie is best at physics, biology, maths and English at school. Her ambition is to work with computers, possibly as a programmer.

Her brother Anthony, eleven, also likes jokes.

'He's not as good as me though,' said Julie modestly. 'Not *really!*'

•

What great dancer has a lot of steps?

Fred Astairs.

•

What adds, subtracts, multiplies and bumps into lights?

A mothematician.

•

What kind of trees have their fortunes read?

Palm trees.

•

What do you call someone who steals rubber bands?

A rubberbandit.

•

What race is everybody in?

The human race.

When is a grape very speedy?

When it's race-in.

●

What's green, has lots of teeth, and holds up your socks?

An alligarter.

●

How many gets can't you remember?

Four (gets).

●

What vegetable always comes first in a race?

The lettuce – it's always a head.

●

What number is also a game?

Ten is.

●

What does a house wear?

Address.

What is green, weighs a ton, and can float in a glass of martini?

An olivephant.

•

Why were old-time kings like books?

Because they had a lot of pages.

•

What do you call spiders who have just got married?

Newly-webs.

•

What do you call a spider who never got married?

A spinster.

How do you count cows?

With a cowculator.

•

Where do sheep do their shopping?

At Woolies.

•

Why do little witches get As at school?

Because they're good at spelling.

•

Why does Metal Mickey like boating?

Because he's a rowbot.

•

What makes a cemetery so noisy?

The coffin.

•

Why did the duck wash its clothes in the ocean?

Because it was full of Tide.

What do you get if you cross a cow with a jumping bean?

Milk shakes.

•

What do you get if you cross an ocean with a kangaroo?

Wet.

•

What do you get if you cross the Atlantic with the *Titanic*?

Half-way.

•

How does the Abominable Snowman impress people?

He puts his beast foot forward.

•

What does a kettle suffer from?
Boils.

•

Where do bees wait for transport?

    At a buzz stop.

•

What cereal does an Eskimo have for
breakfast?

    Snowflakes.

•

What pudding do moaners really enjoy?

    Apple grumble.

•

How many birds with big beaks make a pair?

    Well, toucan!

•

What bird doesn't care if you kill it?

    An owl. It doesn't give a hoot.

•

What do bees say in summer?

    Swarm, isn't it?

How does a musician get home?

    With the key of A flat.

●

What does a policeman eat when he has
arrested someone?

    Irish stew (in the name of the law)!

●

What do you call a ghost that reads meters?

    An inspectre.

●

What did the spook say when it learned
about haunting?

    It just ghost to show!

●

Which wild animal would you find on the
lawn, dressed up in smart clothes?

    A dandelion.

●

What does a famous vampire get through the post?

Fang mail.

•

What tuba can't be played?

A tuba toothpaste.

What sort of instrument did the Ancient Britons play?

The Anglo Saxonphone.

●

What's a vampire's favourite dance?

The vaults!

●

What does the word minimum mean?

A very small mother.

●

What did the second letter of the alphabet say to the third?

Oh I do like to be beside the seaside.

●

What kind of fish is yellow and lonely?

A lemon sole.

●

What do you call the money earned by a vegetarian?

A celery.

●

Why did the driver go into the dressing room?

To change gear.

●

Why is a foot like an old story?

Because it's a legend.

●

What is a polygon?

A parrot that has run away from home.

●

What is a sleeping pill for cattle called?

A bulldozer.

●

What is an ig?

An Eskimo's house that hasn't got a lavatory.

What fruit was a famous rock star?

John Lemon.

•

What is a ghost's favourite day for haunting?

Moanday.

•

What did the ancient Egyptians call their mothers?

Mummy.

•

What does a crusty old vampire call his false teeth?

A new-fang-led invention.

•

Knock knock.
Who's there?
A little boy.
A little boy who?
A little boy who can reach the knocker!

*There was such a bad riot the first time a top hat was ever worn in public that its inventor, James Heatherington, was fined £50 for breach of the peace!*

*The city of Los Angeles used to be called El Pueblo de Nuestra Senora la Reina de los Angeles de Porciuncula.*

# Melanie Giles's Jokes

Melanie Giles is ten, lives in Ampthill with her brother Darren, and goes to Alameda Middle School. She loves reading, and collects jokes from newspapers, comics, books, the library, and other people. She 'got the bug' from Darren when she was about seven.

Mum listens to her jokes as well, and pays the postage when she sends them off to newspapers. Melanie also tries out jokes on her friends – 'and if they don't run away screaming I know they're all right'. Any prize money is shared with her brother.

Other hobbies: reading (lots of books a week), netball, hockey, knitting.

And writing her own stories. Jan Needle look out!

What smells good in a spaceship early in the morning?

Unidentified frying objects!

•

What do ducks watch on television?

Duckumentaries.

•

What has four wheels and flies all around?

A corporation dustcart.

•

What is bought by the yard and worn by the feet?

Carpeting.

•

What is green and goes boing boing boing?

A spring onion.

•

Did you hear about the red sauce chasing the brown sauce?

It couldn't ketchup.

What two kinds of fish do you need to make a pair of shoes?

Soles and eels.

•

How did the octopus go into battle?

Fully armed.

•

How do you get the flies out of your living room?

Put the dustbin in the kitchen!

•

What do jellybabies wear on their feet?

Gum boots.

•

What wears a coat all winter and pants all summer?

A dog.

•

How did the glow-worm feel when it was trodden on?

De-lighted!

●

What is shut when it's open and open when it's shut?

A level crossing.

●

What does a mermaid eat for breakfast?

Toast and mermalade.

●

What is an orphan breakfast food?

One with snap and crackle, but no pop!

●

What is an outside light?

A Chinese footballer!

●

What dog is always in a hurry?

A dash-hound.

What do you call a Russian who doesn't like pop music?

A red square.

·

How do you make a potato puff?

Chase it round the garden.

·

What fish sleeps on the sea bed?

A kipper.

·

What do you call a midget who works down a mine?

A mini miner.

·

What plays the bagpipes while cooking chips?

The Frying Scotsman.

·

Who invented the sword dance?

Someone who wanted to dance and cut his toenails at the same time.

•

What did the cheese biscuits say to the almonds?

You're nuts and we're crackers.

•

What is found in the kitchen and makes your dreams come true?

A wishing machine.

•

'Doctor doctor, I feel like an old tin can.'
'Take this, and you'll soon be full of beans.'

•

How do Red Indians send secret messages?

They use smokeless fuel.

•

What do bees do with their honey?

They cell it.

●

What is the main ingredient of dog biscuits?

Collie-flour.

●

What stands in Paris soaking wet?

The Eiffel Shower.

●

What happens when two snails fight?

They slug it out.

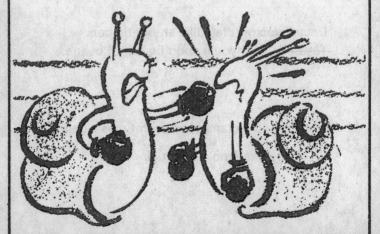

Why did Robin Hood steal from the rich?

> Because the poor had nothing worth taking.

●

Who draws the plans for a rabbit warren?

> The burrow surveyor.

●

Policeman: 'Madam, do you know what gear you were in when you crashed your car?'
Woman: 'Yes officer – a pink blouse, a brown skirt and black shoes.'

●

Have you ever seen a catfish?

> No, but I've seen a horsefly!

●

What does Dracula have for breakfast?

> Dreaded wheat.

●

What's the difference between pack ice and a clothes brush?

> One crushes boats, the other brushes coats.

●

What is the difference between a coyote and a flea?

> One howls on the prairie, the other prowls on the hairy.

●

Why is your dog called Blacksmith?

> Everytime I call him he makes a bolt for the door!

●

Why is your bed in the fireplace?

> Because I sleep like a log.

●

What do you call a skinny Apache?

> A Red Thindian.

●

What is a scribble by an American called?

A Yankee Doodle.

•

What would you use to flatten a ghost?

A spirit level.

•

What did the baby hedgehog say when it bumped into the cactus?

Is that you, Mum!

•

What suffers more than a giraffe with a sore throat?

A centipede with fallen arches.

•

What did the male centipede say to the female centipede?

You've got a nice pair of legs, pair of legs, pair of legs, pair of legs, pair of legs, pair of legs, pair of legs . . .

•

Where do dogs keep their money?

Barklay's Bank.

•

What did one traffic light say to the other?

Don't look now, I'm changing.

•

What animal needs an oilcan?

A squeaking mouse.

•

Why is it hard for a leopard to hide in the jungle?

They are always spotted.

•

Why are a penny and a dog alike?

They both have heads and tails.

•

Why did the ants hurry across the biscuit box?

It said 'Tear along the dotted line'!

•

It is still an offence to whistle in London's Burlington Arcade – or bowl a hoop or a wheel on a London pavement.

Robert Leech, who went over the Niagara Falls in a barrel, died after slipping on a banana skin!

# Jan Needle's Jokes

Jan Needle is forty, lives near Oldham, Lancs, and did very badly at school. He is infamous in several public houses for his jokes, and his hobbies are sailing and canal-boating. He drives a large, shattered, French car and listens to very loud reggae as he goes up and down the motorways.

Because he writes books for children he visits lots of schools and colleges all over Britain. Keep your eyes out for him – he's short, scruffy and incredibly handsome.

●

What do you call a cat with scruffy fur that's just eaten a duck?

A duck-filled tatty puss.

Teacher: 'What's a cubic foot?'
Boy: 'Dunno Miss, but it sounds jolly
painful.'

●

Boy: 'Mum, I don't like cheese with holes in it.'
Mum: 'Well, eat the cheese and leave the
holes on the edge of your plate.'

●

Who was Joan of Arc?

Noah's wife.

●

Grandad: 'How are you getting on at school?'
Grandson: 'Fine thanks. Centre forward in
football and right back in lessons.'

●

What haunts an aeroplane?

An air ghostess.

●

Police notice: Man wanted for burglary.
Apply within!

Who led ten thousand pigs to the top of the hill and then back down again?

The Grand Old Duke of Pork.

•

'Doctor doctor, I keep thinking I'm a brick wall.'
'Don't worry, I'll help you get over it.'

•

What do you call a very thin weightlifter?

Willy Snap.

•

Do you know how to make a firelighter?

Take out all the coal.

•

'Doctor doctor, I feel like a goat.'
'How long has this been going on?'
'Ever since I was a kid.'

•

Where would you find a giant squid?

In a giant's wallet.

Tramp: 'Could you spare a piece of cake, lady?'
Lady: 'Won't bread do?'
Tramp: 'Certainly not, it's my birthday!'

•

What do you get if you dial 666?

A policeman walking on his hands.

•

What animal has two humps and lives at the North Pole?

A very confused camel.

What animal has three humps?

A camel with a rucksack.

●

What other animal has three humps?

A dromedary with two rucksacks!

●

What do you call a camel with three humps?

Humphrey.

●

Turkey to disobedient chick: 'If your father could see you now he'd turn in his gravy.'

●

What book teaches you how to fight?

A scrapbook.

●

Where do baby apes sleep?

In apricots.

'Doctor doctor, I think I'm floating in space!'
'Oh dear, I'll give you a different capsule!'

●

How do you hire a horse?

Put a brick under each leg.

●

How do you hire a car?

Don't try and lift it – it Hertz!

●

What did the cowboy say when his Mum
mended his yellow socks?

Goldarn!

●

What did the earwig say when it fell off the
cliff?

Earwigo!

●

What does a ghost do if its dog loses its tail?

Goes to an off-licence – they retail
spirits!

Why are waiters good at sums?

Because they know their tables.

●

Why are lumberjacks good at harder sums than waiters?

They're used to handling logs.

What does a traffic warden have in his sandwiches?

Traffic jam.

•

What's musical and keeps you dry?

A humbrella.

•

Why are cooks cruel?

Because they batter fish, beat eggs and whip cream.

•

Where did Tarzan get his loin cloth?

At a jungle sale.

•

What's the best way to save your soul?

Walk on your heel.

•

Did you hear about the terrible goalie?

After letting through fifteen goals he put his head in his hands in shame – and dropped it.

Did you hear about the other terrible goalie?

 He dived to catch a bus – and it went
 right under him.

●

Where do whales get weighed?

 At a whaleway station!

●

Did you hear about the two prunes who were
arrested for being stewed?

 They were remanded in custardy.

Who is in charge of the police anti-ghost squad?

>The chief inspectre.

•

What do Poles do in Poland?

>Hold up the telegraph wires.

•

What has one wheel and flies?

>A wheelbarrow full of rotting fruit.

•

What has four legs and flies?

>A dead horse.

•

Teacher: 'Fred, you must learn to give and take.'
Fred: 'But sir! I've just taken his orange and given him a black eye!'

•

Who was the world's first chiropodist?

>William the Corncurer.

Dad: 'Don't you know it's rude to reach out for the cakes? Haven't you got a tongue?'
Daughter: 'Yes, but my arm's much longer!'

●

Why did the farmer steamroller his field?

He wanted to grow mashed potatoes.

●

What's the definition of a milk shake?

A cow doing the Twist.

●

What did the electrician's wife say when he was a long time getting home?

Wire you insulate!

●

What lives underground and is dangerous to tanks?

A mole with a bazooka.

How do you milk a snake?

  With a very low stool.

●

What do you get if you cross an adder and a cow?

  A milk snake.

●

'Knock knock.'
'Who's there?'.
'Mandy.'
'Mandy who?'
'Mandy lifeboats, the ship's sinking!'

●

'Knock knock.'
'Who's there?'
'Little old lady.'
'Little old lady who?'
'I didn't know you could yodel!'

●

What's the fastest thing in the world?

  Milk – it's pasteurised before you see it!

Why are there no horses on the Isle of Wight?

> Because the people there prefer Cowes
> to Ryde!

●

What do you give an excited elephant?

> Trunkquillisers.

●

What is rhubarb?

> Celery with high blood pressure.

●

Why do lazy boys still have to go to school?

> Because school won't come to them.

●

What does the sea say when it reaches the coast?

> Nothing, it just waves.

●

What's big and hairy and flies at twice the speed of sound?

> King Kongcorde.

How did the police catch the wool thief?

> They knew he always worked to a pattern.

●

Teacher: 'Your essay on "our dog" is word for word the same as your sister's.'
Charlie: 'Yes, Miss, it's the same dog.'

●

Where do hangmen buy their ropes?

> At a nooseagent's.

●

What do cats watch on TV?

> Mews at Ten.

●

What do ambitious cats aim for?

> Purrfection.

●

What is the French word for dentures?

> Aperitif.

What is the French for a lawnmower?

> A coup de grace.

●

How do you cook toast in the jungle?

> Under a gorilla.

●

What do you get if you cross an elephant with a musician?

> Tuskanini.

●

What would you call a five-foot judge?

> A small thing sent to try us.

●

What do you get if you cross a football team with a pig?

> Queens Pork Rangers.

●

'Dad, where's the Equator?'
'You'd better ask your mother, son. She puts everything away in this house!'

What do they play at prison discos?

Criminal records.

●

What haunts operating theatres?

Surgical spirits.

●

How do you get rid of a boomerang?

Throw it down a one-way street.

●

Which French artist was short but extremely hygienic?

Two Loos Lautrec!

●

What did the dentist say when his wife baked a cake?

Can I do the filling?

●

Policeman: 'Excuse me, sir, your dog was chasing that man on a bike.'
Owner: 'Naughty Rover! I'll take the bike off him!'

Did you hear about the stupid jellyfish?

It set.

●

What boat is best for shooting rapids?

A gunboat.

●

What do scientists' children get for tea?

Microchips.

Heard about the short-sighted harpoonist?

> He won the Miss Whales competition.

•

Why aren't elephants allowed on beaches?

> In case their trunks fall down.

•

What's pink and slimy and weighs four tons?

> An inside-out elephant.

•

What did Dracula say when he saw
Frankenstein's new girl friend?

> Where did you dig her up?

•

Did you know there is a school for
comedians?

> They have to pass their ho-ho levels.

•

What did the crook say when he was
wrapped in silver paper?

Curses! Foiled again!

•

Did you hear about the deaf cowboy?

He sold his ranch and herd!

•

What happens when you immerse the
human body in hot water?

The phone rings.

•

Why did Napoleon always wear his hat
sideways?

It was military tactics – so that the
enemy wouldn't know which way he
was going!

•

What do you do if you get a peanut stuck in
your ear?

Pour in hot chocolate and it'll come out
a Treet!

What's prickly and goes tick tick?

A clockwork hedgehog.

●

How do you start a flea race?

One, two, flea – GO!

●

What is cold, yellow, and cannot speak a word of English?

A Chinese snowman.

●

What happens to frogs when they break down?

They get toad away!

●

What sort of phone calls do vicars make?

Parson to parson.

●

How did the human cannonball lose his job?

He got fired.

Why did the chicken cross the road?

> Because she saw a man laying bricks
> and wanted to know how he did it!

●

How is a doormat related to a doorstep?

> It's a step farther!

●

How do you start a jelly race?

> Get set!

●

'Waiter, what kind of bird is this I'm eating?'
'A wood pigeon, sir.'
'I thought so – bring me a saw!'

●

Why do traffic lights never go swimming?

> They spend too much time changing.

●

What goes up but can't come down?

> An umbrella in a chimney.

What is brown and hairy and coughs?

A chesty coconut.

•

How are a piano and a tuna fish different?

You can't tuna fish!

•

What animals are members of Weightwatchers?

Fish – they never go anywhere without their scales!

•

What do you get if you cross a potato with an onion?

A spud with watery eyes.

•

What do you get if you cross a hyena with an Oxo cube?

An animal that makes a laughing stock of itself!

London taxi-drivers are still required by law to carry a nose-bag on the side of their cabs.

Some insects can live for a year after having their heads cut off.

What animals didn't go into the ark in pairs?

Maggots – they went in apples.

●

What's black and hairy and surrounded by water?

An oil wig.

●

What is a myth?

A female moth.

●

What fruit do you find on coins?

Dates.

●

What do you get when you cross a fish with an elephant?

Swimming trunks.

●

What's small and green, and does a good turn every day?

A Boy Sprout.

What's got six legs, four eyes, four ears, two heads and a truncheon?

> A mounted policeman.

•

What do you call a crowd of roadworkers falling down a hill?

> A navvylanche!

•

What do you call a skeleton engine driver?

> Casey Bones.

•

Where do they make laws with holes in them?

> The Houses of Polomint!

•

'Mum, why does everyone call me big feet?'

> 'It's just a joke, love. Did you remember to leave your wellies in the garage!'

•

Why is it dangerous to grit the roads?

> It gets in the cats' eyes!

How can you tell a successful farmer?

He's out standing in his field!

•

Who are the best book-keepers?

People who borrow books and never return them.

•

What dashes through the desert carrying a bedpan?

Florence of Arabia.

•

What do you call a cowboy with no money?

Skint Eastwood.

•

When did the first two vowels appear?

Before U and I were born.

•

Why is petrol like the freight found in a ship?

They both make a cargo.

'Doctor, doctor, I feel like a battery.' 'That's all right – we don't charge!'

●

What is the easiest sort of theft?

A safe robbery.

●

What do you call a sick crocodile?

An illigator.

●

What do you call an alligator stuck in the neck of a bottle?

A crokodile!

●

What do you call a bull that has swallowed a bomb?

Abominable!

●

Why did the orange go to the doctor?

It wasn't peeling very well!